Qatna: The History and Legacy of the Ancient Syrian Bronze Age

By Charles River Editors

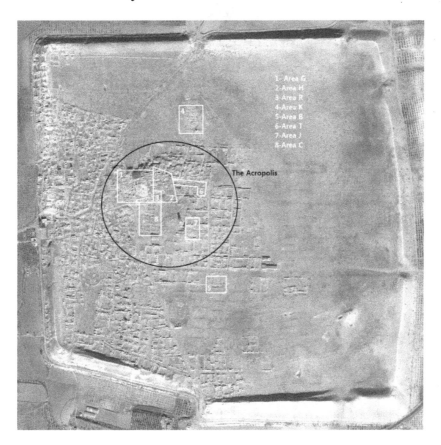

A satellite image of Qatna's ruins

About Charles River Editors

Charles River Editors is a boutique digital publishing company, specializing in bringing history back to life with educational and engaging books on a wide range of topics. Keep up to date with our new and free offerings with this 5 second sign up on our weekly mailing list, and visit Our Kindle Author Page to see other recently published Kindle titles.

We make these books for you and always want to know our readers' opinions, so we encourage you to leave reviews and look forward to publishing new and exciting titles each week.

Introduction

A picture of the royal palace's ruins

The Early Bronze Age in the Near East (c. 3300-2100 BCE) was an era of significant cultural, political, and scientific development. At the same time, city-states became empires, gaining hegemony over the region, and then collapsed, sending Mesopotamia and the Levant into political chaos. The Sumerians were the dominant ethnic group during the first part of the Early Bronze Age Mesopotamia, and the Semitic Akkadians followed them, with the language of the latter became the *lingua franca* of the Near East for more than a millennium. However, as the Early Bronze Age transitioned into the Middle Bronze Age (c. 2100-1550 BCE), new ethnic groups came to prominence that would once more change the region's political composition. These groups ushered in a new era where the Near East's cultural and economic focus shifted from southern Mesopotamia to central and northern Mesopotamia and the Levant.

The primary ethnic group that led this transition was the Amorites, who were originally a collection of nomadic Semitic tribes from the deserts of Arabia. When the Amorites began steadily infiltrating the cities and states of Mesopotamia and Syria around 2000 BCE, they brought a new way of conducting geopolitics in the region while adopting many centuries-old Mesopotamian and Levantine traditions regarding religion literacy and other aspects of culture.

The legendary Hammurabi (r. circa 1792-1750 BCE) descended from the Amorites and most famously established the First Dynasty of Babylon, but other rulers named Hammurabi also reigned in Mari, Assyria, Yamhad, and Qatna. The Kingdom of Qatna, named for the primary city in the kingdom, was located on the other Amorite states' geographical periphery in the northern Levant but was still a significant participant in the Near East's geopolitical system during the Middle Bronze Age. Although researchers know little about the chronological details of the Qatna kings, a combination of sources from Mari, Egypt, and Qatna itself provide an image of the kingdom's place in the world at the time, and it seems Qatna was every bit as powerful as its brother states in Mesopotamia. Thanks to its location, it was able to withstand the aggression of the more powerful states of Assyria and Babylon.

The textual and archaeological evidence shows that Qatna was able to grow and prosper throughout the Middle Bronze Age. As the other Amorite powers collapsed at the onset of the Late Bronze Age (c. 1550-1200 BCE), it was able to stay politically relevant longer by playing the new powers against one another. Eventually, though, Qatna could not stop the march of history, or the armies of Egypt, Mitanni, and Hatti, and Qatna was ultimately leveled, only to be rediscovered over 3,000 years later in the 20th century.

Qatna: The History and Legacy of the Ancient Syrian City during the Bronze Age chronicles the dramatic rise and fall of the Syrian city, and what life was like there. Along with pictures depicting important people, places, and events, you will learn about Qatna like never before.

Early Qatna

Geography has historically played a significant role in the development of cities, kingdoms, and societies. In the pre-modern world, cities that survived were built on defendable ground, near resources such as food and water, and often along or near essential trade routes. The Bronze Age was mostly a period where civilization made great strides. However, only the strongest kingdoms were able to protect themselves because warfare was common, which meant that cities and kingdoms were built using defensible positions. Cities that met more than one prerequisite could advance to the next stages of their development, sometimes becoming the capitals in major kingdoms/empires, as Qatna did.

The modern village of Tel Mishrife, Syria, is approximately where ancient Qatna once stood. The modern town is rather inauspicious and not very important, politically speaking, which is why it was able to conceal an important ancient city for so long. Since there was little reason for Westerners to visit Tel Mishrife, the secrets of ancient Qatna hidden near the modern village remained a mystery. However, Qatna's location in relation to Tel Mishrife was only part of the problem, because, while plenty of ancient texts referenced Qatna, none were too specific about its location. Modern scholars knew that ancient Qatna was located somewhere in Syria or the greater Levant, but finding its precise location proved problematic. Moroever, there was the problem of nomenclature, as Qatna was the name of a city *and* the kingdom that the city controlled, which covered thousands of square miles in modern Syria.

The ancient city of Qatna was located near the Orontes River in the fertile Syrian plain about 15 miles northeast of the modern city of Homs, Syria (Novák, 2004, 299). Qatna's proximity to the Orontes River allowed it to grow economically, as that river and its tributaries were utilized for travel, drinking water, and irrigation. The city was built on a plateau with the innermost section located on an elevated citadel, a position that was needed to protect it from marauding raiders and ambitious kingdoms aiming to add to their kingdoms at Qatna's expense. Qatna's size peaked at about 250 acres during its prime in the Late Bronze Age (Pitard 2001, 31).

Although historians knew of Qatna's existence in the 19th century through Egyptian and Mesopotamian inscriptions and texts, its relatively isolated location remained a mystery until the 1920s. Archaeology in the Levant was spurred in the late 1800s and early 1900s by Westerners' intense interest in biblical studies. British, Americans, Frenchmen, Germans, and others flocked to Palestine, Lebanon, and Syria to locate sites mentioned in the Old Testament and prove the Bible's historicity. Many scholars at that time held divinity degrees and were trained in theological schools throughout the West, and they believed the Old Testament passages were a part of history that could be brought to life with new scientific methods and techniques. While famous sites such as Jericho were located and excavated, other areas were also rediscovered that had as much, if not more bearing, on Biblical and Near Eastern archaeology.

The ruins of Qatna were first excavated by Frenchman Robert du Mesnil du Buisson from

1924-1929. Du Buisson identified three significant structures at the site he labeled the palace, the Temple of Nin-Egal, and the high palace (Novák, 2004, 299-301). Although Du Buisson's categorizations of the structures at Qatna were only partially correct and were later reassessed, which will be more thoroughly discussed below, his work opened up entirely new avenues in the study of the Bronze Age. Thanks to Du Buisson's work, archaeologists now knew the location of one of the region's major powers that contended with Mari, Babylon, and Yamhad.

Despite Du Buisson's work, excavations and work at Qanta lagged for several decades. Studies were interrupted by several factors, most notably World War II, and once archaeology picked back up again in the Middle East in the 1950s, Qatna was largely forgotten in favor of Israel, Lebanon, and Iraq. Even today, the site remains only partially excavated (Kuhrt 2010, 100). Although Hafez al-Assad's government welcomed foreigners and archaeologists to study Syria's pre-Islamic past, wars with Israel and an Islamic uprising in Syria during the late 1970s and early 1980s prevented any significant work at Qatna for several decades. Excavations resumed in 1994 and have continued on and off until the present, but the Syrian Civil War that began in 2011 has limited the work archaeologists can do in the country. In the same vein, the rich material culture from Qatna, particularly from the tomb chamber next to the grand palace, has only recently been made public in exhibitions, most notably at the Metropolitan Museum of Art in New York (Thomason 2009, 53).

Assad

The excavations at Qatna and the material remains found there have helped paint a physical picture of the ancient city, but the texts written during its existence offer the most details about the kingdom's culture, and they are mostly derived from three sources: Qatna itself, the relatively close and contemporary Amorite city-state of Mari, and Egyptian sources.

Initially, the written sources discovered at Qatna were relatively scarce and were, for the most part, limited to inventories and business documents (Redford 1996, 138). Although these sources were useful in understanding business practices and the importance of trade and finance in Qatna, they didn't offer much about the kingdom's political and religious culture or its dynastic chronology. As discussed further below, this meant that historians have had to use synchronistic methods by comparing rulers with known chronologies mentioned in texts from Mari and Egypt to those from Qatna and thereby arrive at approximate dates or at least orders of rule. Of course, that method is not always completely accurate.

In 2002, researchers discovered archives under the royal palace that might eventually offer more details about Qatna's politics, religion, and trade, but most of those are yet to be translated and published. With that said, what has been translated makes clear that Qatna was a powerful kingdom that was deeply involved in foreign affairs during the Middle Bronze Age.

The majority of the texts that concern Middle Bronze Age Qatna come from Mari's extensive cuneiform archives. When Frenchman André Parrot discovered the thousands of tablets in Mari in 1933, they revealed much about not only that city, but about the entire geopolitical system of the region at the time (Pfälzner 2009, 12). The Mari archives contain correspondence letters from and to Mari's kings and those of the major kingdoms of Babylon, Eshnunna, Assyria, Yamhad, Elam, and Qatna, as well as a host of smaller vassal states. It must be remembered that most of these communications were sent to Mari or were intended to be sent from Mari but did not for some reason, or they are copies of letters sent from Mari. Due to all that, the letters are undoubtedly somewhat biased, but they still help explain Qatna's position in the region and reveal a lot about the political dynamics of the period.

The Mari archives are the source of most Middle Bronze Age texts relating to Qatna, and several Egyptian texts document Egyptian-Qatna relations in the Middle and Late Bronze Ages. Qatna's position in the Levant placed it in a unique position since it was influenced as much politically and culturally by Egypt to its south as it was by Mesopotamia to its east or Anatolia to its north. The other major states of the period were either Mesopotamian or Anatolian in their geopolitical and cultural influences.

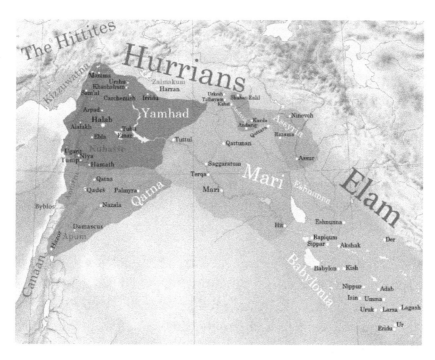

A map of the region in the 18th century BCE

Outside of Mari, the earliest known written reference to Qatna was a fictional text written in

Egypt sometime in the Twelfth Dynasty of the Middle Kingdom (c. 1985-1773 BCE). By the Late Bronze Age, during ancient Egypt's Eighteenth and Nineteenth dynasties (c. 1550-1213 BCE), references to Qatna, or Qedem and Ketne as the Egyptians often referred to it, were much more common. The Qatna-Egypt relationship ebbed and flowed according to how powerful Egypt was at any given time, but the relationship's complexity and depth is not yet fully understood.

Qatna's geographic location is crucial to understanding its development, but the most important factor is the ethnic group that settled and built it. Semitic Canaanite people originally settled the area around Qatna, but after the Ur III Dynasty in Mesopotamia collapsed after 2004 BCE, a new wave of Semitic migrants came to Mesopotamia and the Levant. The new group, known as the Amorites, originated in the Arabian deserts and would begin migrating north, east, and west in independent bands in the mid-3rd millennium BCE (Pitard 2001, 34). The Ur III Dynasty effectively acted as a barrier that prevented the Amorites from infiltrating Mesopotamia, so when it fell, the floodgates into Mesopotamia were opened, which led to a chain effect whereby Amorite tribes entered all lands in the Fertile Crescent, including the Levant (Haywood 2005, 28). The Amorites brought with them a martial spirit that uprooted the old order throughout the Near East, making quick work of the ancient dynasties and sedentary peoples but facing off against each other on numerous occasions. Even after the Amorites settled and became sedentary people themselves, they retained their aggressiveness to a certain extent, which is evident by the regular appearance of walled sites throughout Mesopotamia and northern Syria in the Middle Bronze Age (Redford 1996, 96).

Although the Amorites may have entered Mesopotamia and the Levant as unwanted intruders and war often followed in their initial wake, they eventually adopted their hosts' ways and established new political dynasties. In the process of assimilating into the lifestyles and cultures of the Fertile Crescent's sedentary peoples, they established dynasties in Babylon, Mari, Assyria, Yamhad, and Qatna that were almost culturally indistinguishable from their predecessors. The Amorites worshipped Mesopotamian and Syrian deities, and they even adopted the Akkadian language as their own (Haywood 2005, 32-33). The only vestiges of the past the Amorites retained were their names, suggesting that the Amorite language was never written (Kuhrt 2010, 75).

The process by which the Amorites became sedentary Mesopotamians and Syrians was quite rapid, relatively speaking, and was at least partially made possible due to the existing urbanization in the region. Qatna was already a full-scale city in 2500 BCE, so when the Amorites arrived hundreds of years later, they only had to assert their control over the population (Pitard 2001, 31). From there, once the Amorites made Qatna their city, it did not take long for it to become one of the more influential and powerful states in the region.

Qatna in the Middle Bronze Age

When the Amorite tribes coalesced and formed states in the late 3rd millennium and early 2nd millennium BCE, they developed a geopolitical system that was quite sophisticated for the time. The Late Bronze Age geopolitical system is often referred to as the "Great Powers Club," consisting of Egypt, Hatti, Kassite Babylon, Alashiya (Cyprus), Mitanni, and Assyria, and while that system is much better known, the Amorite states of Mesopotamia and the Levant formed a similar system hundreds of years prior during the Middle Bronze Age. Qatna and the other Amorite states made alliances with each other (often through strategic marriages), claimed vassal states among the smaller and weaker kingdoms in the region, and developed sophisticated trade networks that rivaled any similar system in the pre-modern world.

The precise chronology of Qatna's rulers is a bit of a mystery, but the kings' names are known, and from the Mari archives, historians know the names of Qatna's two rulers during the Middle Bronze Age Amorite geopolitical system: Ishi-Adad and Amut-pi-el. The Mari archives indicate that Ishi-Adad developed an alliance with Amorite Assyria, which was led by Shamsi-Adad (r. circa 1808-1776 BCE) and his son, Ishme-Dagan (r. circa 1775 BCE). Although both considered each other "great kings," Amorite Assyria was more powerful than Qatna, and this was demonstrated in how Ishme-Dagan interacted with Ishi-Adad.

A fascinating letter written by Ishi-Adad to Ishme-Dagan, which never made it to the intended recipient since it was discovered in the Mari archives, indicates that Qatna's king was aware of the unequal status, or at least what he perceived as an unequal status:

> "This matter ought not be discussed; yet I must say it now and vent my feelings. You are a great king. When you placed a request with me for 2 horses, I indeed had them conveyed to you. Yet you, you sent me (just) 20 pound of tin. Without doubt, when you sent me this paltry amount of tin, you had no desire to have honorable discourse with me.

> "Had you planned sending nothing at all – by the god of my father! – I might be displeased! Among us in Qatna, the value of such horses is 600 šekels [= 10 pounds] of silver. But you sent me just 20 pounds of tin! What would anyone hearing this say? Would he not mock us?

> "This house is your house. What is lacking in your house that a brother cannot fulfill the need of his equal? Had you not planned to send me any tin, I might not be upset over it. Are you not a great king? Why have you done this? This house is your house!" (Sasson 2015, 313).

The alliance involved Qatna sending arms and men to aid Assyria (Munn-Rankin 1956, 77), and presumably vice-versa, but it was more often focused on keeping Mari in line. The original

Amorite dynasty that ruled Mari was thrown into turmoil when Sumu-Yaman usurped the throne, but he did not rule very long because Shamsi-Adad quickly swept in and placed one of his sons, Yasmah-Addu (r. circa 1795-1776 BCE), on the throne of Mari (Kuhrt 2010, 98). To ensure that Mari, Qatna, and Ekallatum/Assyria maintained their alliance, Shamsi-Adad arranged for his son to marry Ishi-Adad's daughter, Beltum. Yasmah-Adad was already married to the daughter of Yadhun-Lim, the first king of Mari, and she was his favorite. However, since the Lim line was out of power, the marriage was of no political benefit to Shamsi-Adad, so the Assyrian ruler ordered his son to marry Beltum and make her his primary wife (Mieroop 2007, 109).

Sensing that Beltum was not Yamah-Adad's first choice, Ishi-Adad sent a detailed letter with her to Mari: "I am placing in your lap my flesh and my future. The handmaid (i.e., my daughter) that I give you, may God make her attractive to you. I am placing in your lap my flesh and future, for this House has now become yours and the House of Mari has now become mine. Whatever you desire, just write me and I will give it to you. All over my land, whatever the king (Samsi-Addu) has requested, I myself have never held it back. Why is it that whatever I desire from the king, he does not give it? Let him fulfill request as I fulfill yours." (Sasson 2015, 104).

The marriage marked the beginning of a relationship between Qatna and Mari where one side often committed more resources than the other. The marriage also resulted in an easing of border restrictions between the two kingdoms. It is essential to understand that the ancient Near East's kingdoms and empires had borders similar to the modern concept, which sometimes included border checkpoints, and a letter from Ishi-Adad to Yasmah-Adad indicates that the latter requested to use the former's grazing lands. According to the letter, Ishi-Adad was happy to accommodate his son-in-law: "As soon as you wrote to me, I paid attention to your words. Your sheep and nomads should cross over this way, so that my sheep and yours could graze together. Pasture is very abundant (here). Send me your sheikhs; I will give them instruction and entrust your sheep to them. My sheep and yours should graze together." (Sasson 2015, 105).

Although no other details are provided in the letter and a response letter is yet to be discovered in Qatna, researchers assume that Ishi-Adad received some benefit from the deal. More than likely, Ishi-Adad hoped to gain some military leverage, such as being allowed to post some of his troops in Mari's territory.

That said, other texts indicate that Yasmah-Adad was an inferior partner when it came to military affairs, and many of the letters from Mari depict Yasmah-Adad as a weak and ineffectual ruler compared to his brother. In fact, it seems he was often disparaged by his father (Mieroop 2007, 109). One notorious Mari letter alludes to Yasmah-Adad being regularly scolded by Shamis-Adad, whom he referred to in a submissive manner that is translated into English as "daddy." Part of it reads, "Furthermore, Daddy wrote to me, 'Can you not observe your brother, who leads vast armies? Yet you cannot take charge of your palace and house!' this is what Daddy wrote to me. . . Had I not felt safe in my lord's capital, Daddy could count me as equal to my lord. Now dependable servants and their attendants are at the service of my lord and he is pleased. As for me, since I was young and even now, I have never heard complaints in Daddy's presence. He elevated me, Daddy, and set me (to rule) Mari. . . But now, your god as taken away those associated with me that Daddy gave me. As a result, I now live in Mari, yet my foundations are not secure. Night and day, I keep weeping. Now, however, if my Daddy says 'Come now, I shall secure your foundations so that you can stay in Mari…'" (Sasson 2015, 23-24).

This letter helps put into context the situation Ishi-Adad faced when he dealt with Yasmah-Adad and Mari. Yasmah-Adad was fickle with women, unresponsive with sheep and borders, and generally weak in his father's eyes, but despite these glaringly apparent inadequacies, Ishi-Adad had to deal with Mari's weak ruler to keep Qatna's influence in the region. Influence over Mari meant one less potential enemy to deal with, favorable trade agreements, and the alliance's continuation with the more powerful Shamsi-Adad.

The Mari letters also indicate that despite the fact Mari and Qatna did have a military alliance, Qatna pulled most of the weight on the battlefield and in terms of resources. As much as Yasmah-Adad proved to be unreliable as a sovereign in his father's eyes, he was even more worthless as an ally to Qatna. In one letter, Ishi-Adad has to resort to shame and the invocation of a sacred oath to get reinforcements sent from Mari: "For quite a long time now, I keep on writing about the troops, and (officers for) your troops keep telling me, 'Yes troops are coming up!' Yet, there is no coming up of troops. Now I have once again taken a sacred oath, but until my eyes see (it), I will not believe any troops are coming up." (Sasson 2015, 106). In another letter, Ishi-Adad had to entice Yasmah-Adad with reports of easy pickings and spoils of war to get the Mari ruler to act: "You have sent me good news about Išme-Dagan, and I was very pleased. Another matter: You must not be remiss about sending me news of your coming up here. Time is propitious for your coming up. Feed your troops spoils so they will bless you. These three towns are hardly fortified and we can take them in one day. Come up here quickly and let us capture these towns, so that your troops could 'eat' spoils. If you are my brother, come up here quickly." (Sasson 2015, 187).

Unfortunately, there are no known texts that accompany these accounts, so it remains a question whether these were the same campaigns or if Yasmah-Adad sent the requested reinforcements. Given what is known about Yasmah-Adad, it might be fair to assume that he failed to send any help, and either way, Qatna continued to exert its power in the region while Yasmah-Adad was toppled from power in Mari after his father died, probably in battle (Mieroop 2007, 109).

While Mari experienced a relatively brief period of political chaos before the Lim Dynasty was reestablished, Ishi-Adad was succeeded by Amut-pi-el on the throne in Qatna. As with all of the kings of Qatna, the precise dates of Amut-pi-el's rule are not known, but his rule did overlap with Zimri-Lim's (r. circa 1775-1762) in Mari, so a general timeframe can be deduced.

The primary sources suggest that Amut-pi-el was quite an active leader who engaged in war, diplomacy, and trade with the Near East's other major states, even more so than his predecessor. Once the Near East's political situation changed when Shamsi-Adad and his family were vanquished, the northern Syrian state of Yamhad became Qatna's chief rival, and though there is no documentation to confirm it, Yamhad and Qatna were likely rivals well before that since they were the two major northern Syrian states.

While Shamsi-Adad and his family ruled most of northern Mesopotamia, Qatna was their loyal ally, but Yamhad was an enemy state and relatively isolated. After Shamsi-Adad died and his family's grip on the region was released, Yamhad made its play to become the most powerful kingdom, but Qatna stood in its way. Yamhad and Qatna quarreled repeatedly and eventually went to war, probably over the lucrative trade routes that connected the Levant to Mesopotamia and influence over Mari (Kuhrt 2010, 100). The Qatna-Yamhad conflict eventually ended in a stalemate, with Amut-pi-el and Yarim-Lim, king of Yamhad, concluding a peace treaty, but as with many peace treaties throughout history, the one between Qatna and Yamhad proved to be only a temporary respite between conflicts (Munn-Ranking 1956, 78).

By the early 18th century BCE, the Near East was being influenced by even more kingdoms, including some outside the region. Middle Kingdom Egypt had grown wealthy and militarily powerful enough to develop ties with some states in the Levant, such as Qatna, while to the east of Mesopotamia, Elam began asserting itself more regularly in Mesopotamian and Syrian affairs. Amut-pi-el saw the political benefits of diplomatically engaging these two powers, and while contacts with Egypt proved to be more enduring, relations with Egypt were more impactful in the broader geopolitical picture.

Qatna possibly offered Elam part of its land, or use of its land, in return for an alliance against Yamhad (Mieroop 2007, 101). It is unknown how far the Qatna-Elam alliance progressed because Babylon's Hammurabi eventually established Mesopotamia's most dominant kingdom, but a text from Mari explains how Zimri-Lim attempted to stop it:

> "The city of Mari, the palace, and district are in good order. The Elamite and Qatna messengers have arrived here in transit, having been at the (court of the) Elamite regent. Kukkumanzu, the Elamite messenger, and Ebi-El, the Qatna messenger who is his escort, are heading toward Qatna. I have detained these men. My lord ought to write me promptly whatever his decision -whether they may proceed or should be detained.

> "As to Yarpa-Addu – the messenger of the king of Qatna on a mission to my lord and about whose transfer to my lord I had previously written – upon reflection now, I have decided to detain this man. I was thinking, 'The allied forces may not yet

have fully assembled before my lord, and if I send this man to my lord, he may learn the situation with the army.' For this reason, I have detained him. Now, then, ought I send this man to my lord? Whatever his decision, my lord should write me.

"With regard to Yatar-Addu, I have made enquires of merchants within my own circles, and was told, 'He is well, and nothing is wrong. The day after the (departure of) the messengers of the king of Qatna, they sent this man on a mission, and Innirri is commissioned with him.' I have sent the letter to my lord on the 11th of (month) Igi.kur." (Sasson 2015, 127).

This text demonstrates that the Near East was diplomatically sophisticated, and that the kingdoms also employed espionage and subversion to meet their goals. The power dynamics may have been based on more than just brute military force, but military power still played the most important role.

Qatna and Egypt

The Middle Bronze Age coincided with the Middle Kingdom in Egypt (c. 2055-1650 BCE), which represented the Nile civilization's second great flowering of culture, wealth, and power. The Egyptians of the Middle Kingdom were not quite able to duplicate the monumental building greatness of the Old Kingdom, but they did surpass the earlier Egyptians in terms of foreign influence. The Twelfth Dynasty kings expanded Egyptian influence south, past the first cataract on the Nile River and well into Nubian territory. Archaeological and textual evidence shows that they also had some degree of influence in the Levant.

The Middle Kingdom Egyptian presence in the Levant may have begun under the reign of the Eleventh Dynasty King Montuhotep II (ca. 2008-1957 BCE), who possibly led a small-scale military campaign into the region (Grajetzki 2006, 20). This campaign initiated an Egyptian policy of taking an interest in their northern neighbors, as demonstrated by Egyptian vessels, scarabs, and other material goods being found by modern archaeologists throughout the Levant.

Egyptian scarabs, which are amulets in the form of a scarab beetle that are often inscribed with a particular Egyptian ruler's name, are among the most common pieces of material culture that demonstrate an Egyptian presence in the Levant during the Middle Bronze Age. With that said, some scarabs have been found in cities where there was no official Egyptian presence, so it remains unknown if they were authentic Egyptian pieces or "knockoffs" manufactured in the Levant (Ben-Tor 1997, 168). Egyptian style stone vessels were also distributed widely across the Levant during the Middle Bronze Age, but again, it is unclear how many of these vessels were imported from Egypt or how many were made in the Levant by workmen who emulated the Egyptian style (Braun 2003, 33-34). Egyptian material remains dated to the Middle Bronze Age have also been discovered in Qatna.

The evidence of Egyptian items and contemporary texts didn't fully outline the extent of the relationship between Qatna and Egypt, but du Buisson and the earliest French archaeologists who worked at Qatna in the 1920s were delighted when they discovered a cache of cuneiform tablets along with an Egyptian sphinx dated to the Twelfth Dynasty among the palace's ruins (Novák 2004, 303). The discovery was the first among hundreds of Egyptian and "Egyptianizing" jewelry, scarabs, vessels, and statues that have been discovered in Qatna, which are believed to have come to the kingdom anytime between 2000 and 1800 BCE. Egyptianizing refers to objects made outside of Egypt that emulate authentic Egyptian workmanship. Egyptian artists may have done the work in Qatna, or local artists in Qatna may have trained in the Egyptian style, but in either case they were not originally manufactured in Egypt.

The discovery of these items has led to a debate among scholars about the nature of the relationship between Qatna and Egypt, namely whether the presence of such abundant amounts of Egyptian culture prove Egyptian hegemony over the region or just the existence of extensive trade networks. Based on the evidence, the hypothesis that Egypt dominated the region is not very likely but still should be considered. According to this theory, the Egyptians of the Twelfth Dynasty were able to amass enough resources to build a large army that temporarily occupied parts of the Levant, including Qatna, but there are many reasons complicating potential Egyptian control over the Levant during the Middle Kingdom. Most notably, it would have required vast resources for such an endeavor. During the New Kingdom, when the Egyptians are documented as having control over most of the southern Levant, Egyptian sources explained that the pharaoh had to build garrisons protected by a considerable number of troops and supported by a constant stream of supplies. New Kingdom Egyptians also created many roads that led from Egypt into the Levant, which implies that none of that infrastructure existed during the Middle Kingdom. The Egyptians were quite literate people, and their rulers tended to detail all of their successful military campaigns, so the fact that none of the annals from the Middle Kingdom concern military campaigns into the Levant suggests that they did not exert military control over that region.

However, there is anecdotal evidence that suggests Egypt controlled Qatna and other parts of the Levant. An Egyptian text mentions a military campaign conducted by the Twelfth Dynasty king, Senusret III (r. circa 1878-1842 BCE), into the land of Sekhem, which is generally equated by modern scholars with the Biblical Shechem (Redford 1996, 76). The classical historians Diodorus, Herodotus, and Manetho all seem to corroborate this campaign in their writings, as they chronicled how an Egyptian king named "Sesostris" (the Greek version of the name Senusret) conquered "Asia." According to Herodotus, "Sesostris, the priests said, sailed first with a fleet of warships from the Arabian gulf along the coast of the Indian Ocean, subduing the coastal tribes as he went, until he found that shoal water made further progress impossible; then on his return to Egypt (still according to the priests' account) he raised a powerful army and marched across the continent, reducing to subjection every nation in his path. Whenever he encountered a courageous enemy who fought valiantly for freedom, he erected pillars on the spot inscribed with his own name and country, and a sentence to indicate that by the might of his armed forces he had won the victory." (Herodotus, *The Histories*, II, 102).

While it is unlikely that Senusret III or other Twelfth Dynasty rulers embarked on a far-ranging military campaign like the one described by Herodotus, the presence of these texts suggests that the Egyptians conducted at least one or more minor military campaigns into the Levant. And obviously, the archaeological evidence from Qatna heavily suggests there was an Egyptian presence there, if not a military one.

In addition to the Egyptian objects initially discovered in Qatna in the 1920s, more recent excavations have found even more products from the Nile Valley. A German-Syrian archaeological expedition uncovered more than 60 Egyptian and *Egyptianizing* stone vessels from the palace's royal tomb in 2002 (Ahrens 2006, 15). Among the Egyptianizing pieces in Qatna, many have been identified as almost certainly having an Egyptian provenance.

A serpentinite vase with the Twelfth Dynasty king's name, Amenemhat III (r. circa 1831-1786), written in a cartouche, is among the more interesting discoveries. The text on the vessel references the crocodile god Sobek of Shedet, which suggests it was probably initially made and used in the Sobek Temple in Shedet, Egypt (Ahrens 2006, 20). Other notable Egyptian pieces recently found in Qatna include a royal sphinx and fragments of statues found in the royal palace (Ahrens 2006, 26-27).

There is no doubt that the objects are Egyptian in style, and many, such as the vase of Sobek, can almost certainly be traced directly to a workman's shop in Egypt, but the context of their placement raises more questions than answers. They may have been royal gifts used by the royals of Qatna for mundane purposes, or they could have been status symbols used by the Qatna elite to show their connection to the powerful kingdom to the south. The presence of these Egyptian objects in Qatna also brings up the simple yet essential question of how they got to the city.

Although one or more Egyptian kings likely conducted a military campaign into the Levant during the Middle Bronze Age, which may have entered the Kingdom of Qatna, there is no evidence that a long-lasting occupation ensued. No evidence from Egypt suggests that the Egyptians developed a well-regulated empire in the Levant as they did in the New Kingdom, nor do the Egyptian objects discovered in Qatna prove large-scale or enduring occupation. One possibility is that the items were brought to Qatna after the Middle Kingdom collapsed (Ahrens 2006, 26) by Egyptian or Canaanite refugees. In this scenario, elites in Egypt and Canaanites who had lived in Egypt for some time fled when the political situation in Nile Valley became untenable and central authority collapsed. Qatna apparently retained its political stability at the time and welcomed the wealth and potentially the skills of refugees fleeing Egypt.

There are a few other possibilities for how Egyptian material goods ended up in Qatna. The most plausible theory is that Egypt's Twelfth Dynasty kings gave the items to the Qatna kings as prestige gifts, making them symbols of ostentatious wealth (Ahrens 2006, 27). Another possibility is that some of the Egyptian goods discovered in Qatna, or even most of them, were made by artists in Qatna who emulated Egyptian styles (Frankfort 1996, 243-4). Egyptianizing art has been discovered throughout the Near East, and across the region, gods, goods, and even artistic styles often traveled great distances and found new homes. Egyptianizing art has been found throughout the Levant, as have Greek and Persian works.

Since there is a relatively large amount of Egyptian or Egyptianizing artifacts discovered in Qatna, there is a real possibility that a combination of all these factors contributed. The Egyptians may have invaded the Levant and left some items in Qatna, while also leaving behind emissaries. Once the Middle Kingdom collapsed, refugees brought more Egyptian goods, and by that time, artists in Qatna had learned to emulate Egyptian artistic styles.

There were very few mentions of Qatna in Egyptian texts before the Late Bronze Age, and most were fleeting, but one is worthy of closer attention. The first known mention of Qatna other than the Mari archives is in a fictional Egyptian tale known as *The Story of Sinuhe*. The story is more historical fiction or pseudo-history than a purely fictional story, as it concerns known historical figures and one significant historical event. The story is believed to have been written during the reign of Twelfth Dynasty King Senusret I (c. 1956-1911 BCE), and it tells how Amenemhat I (r. circa 1985-1956 BCE) was murdered in a palace conspiracy. Fearing that he would be unjustly implicated in the scheme and face Amenemhat's son and successor's wrath, Senusret I, the noble Sinuhe fled to the Levant to live among the "Asiatics" (as the Egyptians generally referred to the Canaanites and other inhabitants of the Levant).

The story relates how Sinuhe first went to the coastal city of Byblos before moving to Qatna (Egyptian Qedem), where he became a trusted advisor of the king:

> "Land gave to land. I traveled to Byblos; I returned to Qedem. I spent a year and a half there. Then Ammunenshi, the ruler of Upper Retenu, took me to him, saying to me: 'You will be happy with me; you will hear the language of Egypt.' He said this because he knew my character and had heard of my skill, Egyptians who were with him having borne witness for me. (Lichtheim 2006, 224-5)

Sinuhe lives among the people of Qatna and builds a nice life for himself among the elites of the land. But like any true Egyptian, Sinuhe longed to return to the Nile Valley.

Sinuhe was eventually given amnesty by Senusret I, who acknowledged that Sinuhe traveled through Retenu, the ancient Egyptian term for the Levant, and eventually Qatna. The story reads:

This decree of the King if brought to you to let you know: That you circled the foreign countries, going from Qedem to Retenu, land giving you land, was the counsel of your own heart. What had you done that one should act against you? You had not cursed, so that your speech would not be reproved. You had not spoken against the counsel of the nobles, that your words should have been rejected. . . Come back to Egypt! See the residence in which you lived! Kiss the ground at the great portals, mingle with the courtiers! For today you have begun to age. You have lost a man's strength. Think of the day of burial, the passing into reveredness.'" (Lichtheim 2006, 224-5).

It was undoubtedly a tough decision to make to leave Qatna and a position as the king's right hand for an uncertain life as a courtier in Egypt, but Sinuhe was a true Egyptian, so when he heard that the pharaoh had granted him amnesty, he returned to Egypt, never again to see Qatna.

While that was a fictional story, evidence from Egypt suggests that by the end of the Middle Kingdom, Sinuhe would only have been one of many people from Qatna who migrated to Egypt. During the height of the Middle Kingdome, there was an influx of ethnic Amorite immigrants and prisoners of war (Redford 1996, 78-79), some of whom were presumably from Qatna. The wave of migrants could suggest that the invasion hypothesis has some validity and that the Twelfth Dynasty kings campaigned in Qatna and the Levant, but that still wouldn't prove the Egyptians occupied the region for any considerable time. Furthermore, the Middle Kingdom's collapse hypothesis also has standing. Just as Amorite and Canaanite migrants flooded into Egypt during the height of the Middle Kingdom, their ancestors would have journeyed back to Qatna when Egypt descended into anarchy, taking Egyptian materials and culture with them in the process.

Qatna's Culture

Since Egypt is better known and was more enduring and influential than Qatna, it stands to reason that much of the academic and popular focus on Qatna has been on the Egyptian artifacts discovered in the city. The fact that Qatna was not comprehensively studied until recently also plays a role in this perception, but the excavations at Qatna have revealed it to be among the largest and most impressive sites in the Near East during the Middle Bronze Age. In conjunction with that, the excavations have shed light on the kingdom's culture, and how it compared and contrasted with neighbors.

As with many ancient sites, one of the most informative places is the royal palace. As was already mentioned, Qatna was located on an elevated plain, and the royal palace and other important structures were located on an acropolis, much like other important sites in the ancient world. Du Buisson identified two palaces and a temple in his initial excavations, although those identifications have been reassessed in recent years.

The main palace was partially uncovered in the 1920s, but as work at the site resumed in the 1990s, it became apparent just how large it was. The main palace measured about 440 feet by 328 feet, which made it one of the largest buildings in the Levant in the Bronze Age (Novák, 2004, 301). It would have taken immense amounts of resources, manpower, and specialists to build such a large palace, indicating that Qatna was among the era's wealthiest kingdoms. The Mari tablets hinted at Qatna having a considerable amount of diplomatic and military pull in the region, and the size of the palace suggests the kingdom also had a substantial amount of economic power.

Du Buisson identified a second building as the "Temple of Nin-Egal," although decades later, it was determined that the "temple" was the largest building in the great palace. Today the "temple" is known as "Hall C," and it is believed to have served as a monumental hall. Hall C measures 121 by 121 feet, with its roof probably being covered by cedar beams from the nearby Lebanon Mountains (Novák 2004, 303-4). The hall was likely where the kings of Qatna entertained and impressed foreign emissaries. During important events, it would have been filled with courtesans and nobles and decorated with all sorts of exotic art, some of which would have been the Egyptian pieces described above. The palace would have hosted important diplomatic events and would have been the place where economic deals were made and where alliances were forged, making it the nerve center of Qatna.

More traces of the palace's opulence can be found through the remains of a fresco from "Room N" that demonstrates a possible Aegean influence. Elephant bone deposits were also discovered in two other rooms, which at first glance may seem strange, but it is important to remember that ivory was a high-value commodity in the pre-modern world used to create items of conspicuous consumption (Pfälzner 2009, 16-17). Elephant tusks were used to make jewelry and other small items, while the bones were kept for later use, possibly including ritual purposes. The context of the bones being discovered in the great palace may seem strange, but it is logical when one considers the utility of palaces in the Bronze Age.

A number of rooms located on the edge of the palace have been determined to be workshops, which explains why the elephant bones were found in the palace (Bonacossi 2007, 225). Many Bronze Age palaces were built as multi-use facilities. Similar to the Bronze Age palace at Mari, Qatna's great palace had storage rooms, quarters for the royal guards, quarters for foreign emissaries, religious/cult rooms, and rooms meant for the royal family. The layout of Qatna's great palace resembled the Babylonian model more than other Syrian/Levant palaces (Novák 2004, 306). This may have been a result of the Amorite ethnic heritage the Qatna royals shared with their counterparts in Mesopotamia, as opposed to the primarily Canaanite background that was dominant in the Levant. The great palace served as the nerve center of the kingdom, but a "lower city palace" was built later, presumably after Qatna grew in size and influence (Bonacossi 2007, 229).

Archaeologically speaking, the palace's crown jewel was the royal tomb, which connected to the palace's primary residence rooms (Novák 2004, 304). Since excavations at Qatna resumed in 1994, the royal tomb discoveries have provided scholars with a wealth of information. Among the items discovered in the royal tomb were hundreds of vases and other vessels, jewelry, and other fine pieces of art that can be considered "status symbols" (Pfälzner 2009, 17). Although researchers have yet to uncover any religious texts from Qatna that concern the afterlife, the royal tomb, particularly the goods discovered there, clearly point towards a belief in life after death. The royal tomb was not open to the public - only the gods would have seen what was there - so the items were likely meant as offerings to the gods or for the deceased to take into the afterlife.

Another element of the palace that remains somewhat of a mystery is its age. Most historians believe that since Qatna played such a crucial role in the so-called "Mari Age" during the Middle Bronze Age, Qatna's apex of power would have come during that period, and that makes it likely the grand palace was probably first built in the late 18th century or early 17th century (Novák 2004, 309). This opinion is standard among scholars and is based on historical context and archaeological analysis. Still, Bonacossi believed the palace was built up to 300 years later during the Middle Bronze Age/Late Bronze Age transition and was not the residence for the first two known Qatna kings (Bonacossi 2007, 232-6). Unless a text is discovered that definitively gives credit to the king who commissioned the site's building, the matter will probably never be truly settled, but both agree that the construction of the palace, like the city of Qatna itself, was a long-term project that involved immense resources.

The great palace of Qatna was situated on an acropolis presumably for defensive purposes, but the location was also symbolic because the royal family and the most important religious sites were located closer to the gods and far above the majority of the city's inhabitants. Below the palace was the city proper, little of which has been excavated to date, but one of the most impressive elements of the city discovered other than the palace is an earthen rampart that surrounded the site. The rampart stood nearly 60 feet high and was 60 feet wide in some places, with four gates that allowed access into the city. The lower city itself comprised more than 270 acres, and since the layout of Qatna's great palace more closely resembled its Bronze Age counterparts in Babylon and Mari, it is reasonable to assume that the lower city did (Bonacossi 2007, 221).

Qatna's lower city would have contained most of the city's markets and barracks for the army. Foreign merchants would have been allowed to use the markets, but everyone entering the city would have been checked at the gates. In addition to foreign merchants and diplomats who visited Qatna, the city would have also attracted pilgrims to its religious temples.

The lack of textual evidence from Qatna means that there are gaps of knowledge regarding the kingdom's religion, but it can be assumed that owing to their geographic location, the people of

Qatna worship a combination of Mesopotamian and Canaanite/Syrian deities. Texts from the Late Bronze Age mention Shingi as one of the city's most important gods, and Astarte, El, and Baal/Hadad were probably among the most revered. Hadad, who was known as "Baal" among the Canaanites, was the primary deity of Qatna and possibly among all the Amorite states, as can be seen by the number of kings who invoked the name of the god as part of an honorific in their own names. Specific details about mythology and religious rituals may be revealed when more texts from Qatna are translated and published.

One aspect of Qatna's culture that historians know a bit more about is the concept of kingship in the kingdom, and again, parallels can be drawn from other Amorite states found in the early 2nd millennium BCE. The king of Qatna and the kings of other Amorite states were imbued with immense divine power, but they were not considered divine themselves. Technically speaking, the gods were the heads of state, but the kings carried out their commands and ruled at their leisure (Munn-Rankin 1956, 70). As such, the people of Qatna believed that the gods chose their kings and could also vanquish their kings, so the people would view Qatna's loss on the battlefield or the death of the king, whether by disease or assassination, as the gods' will (Munn-Rankin 1956, 71).

The final cultural aspects to examine about Middle Bronze Age Qatna are perhaps what made the kingdom so powerful: diplomatic relations with other kingdoms and trade. Some of the diplomatic maneuvering by Qatna's first two known kings has already been covered above, but it is important to delve a bit deeper into the concept. Essentially, Qatna and the other major kingdoms of the Middle Bronze Age Near East built a diplomatic system whereby alliances constantly shifted and vassal states were often caught in the middle of the larger states' conflicts. Except for Shamsi-Adad's major campaign that took northern Mesopotamia and Hammurabi of Babylon's conquest of nearly all of Mesopotamia, large-scale wars appear to have been the exception, not the rule; the great states preferred to use a combination of coercion and diplomacy, with Qatna excelling in diplomacy and rarely having to use the full force of its military. Qatna was so successful in that regard that it outlived the other major Amorite states of the era.

Qatna's diplomatic influence was tied directly to its success in trade and finance, and there were plenty of people around to conduct such trade. The early 2nd millennium BCE featured the Amorite kingdoms of Mari, Babylon, Assyria, and Qatna, as well as the kingdoms of Larsa and Eshnunna. Kingdoms on the periphery that had diplomatic or commercial contacts with one or more of these powers included Elam, Middle Kingdom Egypt, various kingdoms in Anatolia, and Minoan Crete. Several smaller states scattered throughout the region, and sometimes within the larger states' borders, were Emar, Tunip, Mukish, and Carchemish, among others.

One of the Mari letters details how the system worked during the reign of Amut-pi-El of Qatna: "No king is truly powerful just on his own: ten to fifteen kings follow Hammurabi of

Babylon, as many follow Rim-Sin of Larsa, as many follow Ibal-pi-El of Ešnunna, and as many follow Amut-pi-El of Qatna; but twenty kings follow Yarim-Lim of Yamḫad." (Sasson 2015, 82). This text specifies the region's major powers, and the names that are missing suggest they were lesser powers and/or vassal states.

It is difficult to say for sure what being a vassal entailed or how vassal states were administered, but researchers believe they probably resembled those of the Late Bronze Age Near East, albeit on a smaller scale (Munn-Rankin 1956, 103). The vassal states would have been required to send an annual tribute of specific commodities and may have been expected to send troops in the event of war. Vassal states also occasionally went to war against and made treaties with each other, as demonstrated by an Akkadian language treaty between Alalakh and Tunip's vassal states (Pritchard 1992, 531-2). Despite enjoying a certain level of freedom, the vassal states were still politically inferior to the major states listed above, and most rebellions would end miserably for the vassal state. Remarkably, few texts from the era concerned rebellions, although this does not necessarily mean that it never happened - it could be that rebellions were considered taboo or embarrassing, and thus not worth mentioning.

The diplomatic maneuvering that took place in Qatna and the other major kingdoms was fairly intricate and involved specific protocols and rituals. Each kingdom sent one or more ambassadors/emissaries to the other kingdoms to live at court for extended periods. Since long-distance communication was quite limited at the time, it is believed that the ambassadors were well versed in the political situation before embarking on their assignments and were given a fair amount of leeway on how to act and what types of treaties they could conclude (Munn-Rankin 1956, 103). Emissaries were also present at the capitals of kingdoms for which they were in conflict. For example, Qatna had an emissary in Mari even while Qatna was trying to politically outmaneuver that kingdom, so emissaries from Yamhad and other hostile kingdoms could likely have been found in Qatna at any time.

Although emissaries may have carried the majority of the diplomatic weight, the Amorite states' kings occasionally had direct contact with each other. Alliances and treaties were sealed by oaths, which in the ancient Near East was a sacred affair. A divine witness was always "present" when two kings made an oath, which concluded with the sacrifice of an animal (Munn-Rankin 1956, 103). The Amorite states during the Middle Bronze Age were also more practically bound to each other through diplomatic marriage, not to mention the fact they shared many cultural attributes. Marriages were intended to produce political leverage by creating alliances, gaining favorable trade status, and discouraging others from attacking states involved in the arrangements (Munn-Ranking 1956, 84). Among the best known of these diplomatic marriages was the one between Zimri-Lim, the king of Mari, and Shibtu, the daughter of Yamhad's king, Yarim-Lim. The marriage tie that bound together Ishi-Adad of Qatna and Yasmah-Adad of Mari was discussed previously, but there were no known diplomatic marriages made between Qatna and the other states after the Lim Dynasty returned to power in Mari.

The Amorite states made diplomatic connections with each other, which they utilized to develop trade routes across the region. Qatna was at the western terminus of a major trade route that ran from Mari in the east, through the Syrian desert to Tadmor (later known as Palmyra) before finally ending/beginning in the east at Qatna (Pitard 2001, 40). Although Qatna was not located on the sea, it was relatively close to Ugarit and Byblos' major ports.

Qatna imported tin from Mari and finished products from Mesopotamia, but it was probably a net exporter of goods during the height of its power (Kuhrt 2010, 101). Qatna bred some of the finest horses, and the demand for horses greatly increased as the knowledge of horse domestication, the wheel, and the chariot spread throughout the Near East in the Middle Bronze Age. Qatna had a near monopoly on the timber used for construction since modern Lebanon's famed cedars were located within Qatna's territory, and Qatna was also the entrepot of vases, copper, fabrics, and garments originally manufactured in Cyprus and the Levant intended for the kingdoms of Mesopotamia (Malamat 1971, 12). Egyptian goods also flowed through Qatna before moving north into Syria and west into Mesopotamia.

Many Egyptian scarabs dated to the early 2nd millennium BCE were discovered recently in Terqa, Mesopotamia. Since Terqa was part of the Mari Empire at that time, it appears that even Egyptian goods flowed through Mari, but where the scarabs ultimately originated is a source of debate. One might assume that they came to Mari from Egypt via Qatna, but it is equally probable that they were manufactured in Qatna and then traded, eventually making their way to Terqa (Ahrens 2010, 439). Whether the scarabs were manufactured in Qatna or came there through trade with the Egyptians is not as important as the role Qatna played in the Middle Bronze Age economic system.

Qatna in the Late Bronze Age

Once the Middle Bronze Age transitioned into the Late Bronze Age, the diplomatic system the Amorite states built collapsed, even as some kingdoms like Qatna continued to play an important role in the Near East until the end of the Bronze Age. Although scholars generally place the beginning of the Late Bronze Age at 1550 BCE, there is no hard date for the transition from the Middle Bronze Age to the Late Bronze Age in the Near East, and the transition did not necessarily mark too many technological advances. Perhaps the most notable technological advances during the transition were the widespread diffusion of the chariot and the composite bow, which new kingdoms used to wipe away the old Amorite empires of the Middle Bronze Age.

The Hittite Old Kingdom formed in the mid-17th century under King Hattusilis I (r. circa 1650-1620), marking the beginning of the end for Yamhad. Around the same time, the Amorite First Dynasty of Babylon collapsed under the rule of Samsuditana (r. circa 1625-1595 BCE), sending most of Mesopotamia into a period of chaos. When the Late Bronze Age began, the Hittites were the primary power in Anatolia. Simultaneously, the Kingdom of Mittani ruled Assyria and northern Syria, and the two kingdoms and later New Kingdom Egypt contended for control over the Levant.

Qatna's kings during the Late Bronze Age quickly learned that the role they were accustomed to playing would be significantly diminished in the new geopolitical order. Inscriptions from Qatna list the names of the city's Late Bronze Age kings, but no precise chronology is given, and except for Idanda and Akizzi, they are not known from any other source (Novák 2004, 312). The names and possible order of Qatna's Late Bronze Age rulers are Naplimma, Sinadi, Haddu-nirari, Idanda, and Akizzi. These kings ruled Qatna after it had been circumscribed from what it once was in the Middle Bronze Age, relegated to a second-tier kingdom in the Late Bronze Age. The city-states of Qatna, Qadesh, and Tunip formed a Levantine triangle that served as a political buffer zone between Hatti, Egypt, and Mitanni (Pitard 2001, 43).

By this period, Qatna had no real hope of returning to the power it once had, but it could still maneuver itself among the greater powers to gain a more advantageous position, and excavations from the royal tomb in Qatna show that the kings of Qatna continued to have a relationship with the Egyptians. Among some of the remains of New Kingdom Egyptian material culture discovered in Qatna, a calcite jar with the name of Ames-Nefertari inscribed on it is one of the more interesting (Ahrens 2006, 20). Ames-Nefertari was a queen and God's Wife of Amun – the most important religious position an Egyptian woman could hold, which was equivalent to being a high priestess – so the find certainly deserves consideration. As with the Egyptian Middle Kingdom artifacts discovered in Qatna, it is difficult to say for sure when the jar of Ames-Nefertari arrived at the palace or the context in which the objects were used. Ames-Nefertari lived during the early Eighteenth Dynasty, but the Egyptians did not expand into the Levant until Thutmose III's reign (r. circa 1479-1425 BCE). Thus, the jar was likely taken to the palace as a gift symbolizing Egypt bringing Qatna back into its sphere of orbit (Ahrens 2006, 28-29).

Thutmose III is considered by many to be Egypt's "Caesar" due to at least seventeen military campaigns he led into the Levant during his reign. The campaigns were commemorated in hieroglyphic inscriptions on the columns and walls of the Karnak Temple in Thebes, with Qatna (Ketne) being mentioned in a fragmentary inscription on the eighth campaign (Breasted 2001, 2:237). A pictorial relief from Egypt dated to Amenhotep II's reign (r. circa 1427-1400 BCE) depicts a line of Levantine prisoners from Aleppo, Retenu, Kadesh, and Qatna being led away after another successful Egyptian military campaign (Breasted 2001, 2:314). The Egyptians' repeated campaigns into Qatna's former territory were sometimes met with resistance by Mitanni, but by the late 15th century Qatna no longer offered any resistance.

The Amarna letters are a collection of 383 cuneiform tablets discovered in the Egyptian village of Amarna in 1887 (Moran 1992, xiii-xv). The letters, which were written in the *lingua franca* of the era, Akkadian, detail how the major Near Eastern powers – Egypt, Hatti, Mitanni, Babylon, Alashiya/Cyprus, and later, Assyria – interacted with each other, and they revealed that the geopolitical system the Great Powers built was quite complex. On the political tier below the major powers were the minor powers, including Tunip, Qadesh, Ugarit, Byblos, and Qatna, among others.

Qatna and the other minor powers had to comport themselves as subordinates and could never challenge the major powers directly, but it would make sense that they preferred having certain major powers rule over them compared to others. Qatna's ruins strongly suggest that it may have preferred Egyptian rule, but the city fell more and more into the orbit of the Mitanni and Hittites. Qatna was likely controlled by Mitanni as early as the mid-15th century, but the Hittites were constantly interfering and threatening to conquer the region. At the time, the Kingdom of Mitanni was on equal, if not greater, footing than Hatti, so the Hittites could not expect to conquer and hold Qatna.

Given this situation, it seems that the Hittites were able to influence Qatna and its position vis-à-vis the other major powers behind the scenes. The Hittites may have removed Qatna's King Haddu-nirari and replaced him with Idanda. The details concerning how the Hittites accomplished this remain unknown, but it likely came after Idanda approached the Hittites with the idea. As mentioned above, the rulers of Late Bronze Age Qatna were known to take advantage of the conflicting Great Powers by favoring one over the others.

Idanda probably was not on the Qatna throne very long, though, as he was defeated by the Mitanni King Tushratta (r. circa early to mid-1300s BCE), and it appears that Tushratta replaced Idanda with Akizzi, who was probably the last king of Qatna (Novák 2004, 313). Little is known about Akizzi's reign, but based on some of the Amarna letters, it appears he was politically astute. A letter from Akizzi of Qatna demonstrates that he preferred Egyptian hegemony over his land, though he does not specify why: "Say to the king of Egypt: Message of Akizzi, your servant. I fall at the feet of my lord, my Storm-god, 7 times. Inspect, my lord, his tablets. [He/you will find] the houses of Qatna belong to my lord a[lone]." (Moran 1992, EA 52, 123).

It is unclear exactly why Akizzi attempted to choose Egyptian overlordship over Mitanni since the Mitanni Empire was more of a federation of states than a centrally controlled empire that a king ruled with an iron fist (Kuhrt 2010, 296). It could be that Qatna identified more with the Egyptians after having had contact with them intermittently since the Middle Bronze Age, and Qatna's rulers possibly preferred their culture and style of rule to the Mitanni style.

It may also have been that Akizzi knew what lay in store for Qatna. Tushratta was the last great leader of Mitanni, and after his rule things quickly unraveled in that Syrian kingdom. Internal divisions within the Mitanni royal house greatly weakened the kingdom, and to the north, the Hittites under Suppiluliumas I (r. circa 1344-1322) were expanding their borders south, beyond the Taurus Mountains into the Levant. The Hittites began picking away Mitanni's peripheral possessions, which put Qatna directly in their path.

Knowing that it was only a matter of time before the Hittites arrived in Qatna, Akizzi appealed to the Egyptian King Akhenaten (r. circa 1364-1347 BCE):

> "Say to Namḫurya, the son of the Sun, my lord: Message of Akizzi, your servant. I fall at the fee to my lord 7 times.

> "My lord, I am your servant in this place. I see the path to my lord. I do not desert my lord.

> "From the time my ancestors were your servants, this country has been your country, Qatna has been your city, (an) I belong to my lord.

> "My lord, when the troops and chariots of my lord have come here, food, strong drink, oxen, sheep, and goats, honey and oil, were produced for the troops and chariots of my lord. Look, there are my lord's magnates; my lord should ask them…

> "My lord knows it. My lord [. . .] his ancestors [. . .]. But now the king of Ḫa[tti] has sent them up in flames. The king of Ḫatti has taken his gods and the fighting men of Qatna. . .

> "My lord, your ancestors mad (a statue of) Šimigi, the god of my father, and because of him became famous. Now the king of Ḫatti ahs taken (the statue of) Šimigi, the god of my father. My lord knows what the fashioning of divine statues is like. Now that Šimigi, the god of my father, has been reconciled to me, if, my lord, it *pleases* him, my he give (me) a *sack* of gold, just as much as is needed, for (the statue of) Šimigi, the god of my father, so they can fashion it for me." (Moran 1992, EA 55, 127-8).

Akkizi's attempt to move Qatna into Egypt's sphere of influence was well-conceived, but it came at the wrong time. Akhenaten is known today as a domestic religious reformer, and while he was no pacifist, his exploits in the Levant did not rise to the level of his predecessors. Ultimately, he made no serious attempt to check the Hittites' aggression, a decision that was disastrous for Qatna.

Once it became apparent the Kingdom of Mitanni was plagued with internal dissension, Suppiluliumas led a major campaign that resulted in the destruction of Washukanni, Mitanni's capital, and the envelopment of all Mitanni territories in Syria and the Levant into the Hittite realm of influence. A Hittite treaty text relates how Suppiluliuma laid waste to Qatna's former rival of Halab (Aleppo) before moving south and wiping out every Mitanni aligned city in its path before reaching Qatna: "I turned around and (re)crossed the Euphrates. I vanquished the country of Halba and the country of Mukis. . . Together with their charioteers and their foot soldiers they entered into a conspiracy with Akiya, the king of Arahti. They occupied Arahti and rebelled; this is what they said: 'Let us battle with the great king, the king of the Hatti land!' I, the great king, the king of the Hatti land, vanquished them at Arahti. I took prisoner Akiya, the king of Arahti, Akit-Tessub, Akuwa's brother, and their mariyannu, to the Hatti land. I also brought Qatna with its possessions and all that they owned to the Hatti land." (Pritchard 1992, 318).

After Suppiluliumas's conquest of the Levant, Qatna ceased to be an important city and was rarely mentioned in texts. Meanwhile, the Egyptian kings of the early Nineteenth Dynasty, especially Ramesses II (r. circa 1290-1224 BCE), attempted to claim hegemony over the entire Levant, including Qatna and the Orontes Valley (Breasted 2001, 3:162). The Egyptians and Hittites would engage in an epic battle during Ramesses II's fifth year of rule near the city of Qadesh, but by then, the once great city of Qatna had been relegated to backwater status, destined to be almost entirely forgotten for over 3,000 years.

Online Resources

<u>Other books about ancient history by Charles River Editors</u>

Bibliography

Ahren, Alexander. 2006. "A Journey's End – Two Egyptian Stone Vessels with Hieroglyphic Inscriptions from the Royal Tomb at Tell Mišrife/Qaṭna." *Ägypten und Levante/ Egypt and the Levant* 16: 15-36.

———. 2010. "The Scarabs from the Ninkarrak Temple Cache at Tell 'Ašara/Terqa (Syria):History, Archaeological Context, and Chronology. *Ägypten und Levante/ Egypt and the Levant* 20: 431-444.

Ben-Tor, Daphna. 1997. "The Relations between Egypt and Palestine in the Middle Kingdom as Reflected by Contemporary Canaanite Scarabs." *Israel Exploration Journal* 47: 162-189.

Bonacossi, Daniele Morandi. 2007. "The Chronology of the Royal Palace of Qatna Revisited: A Reply to a Paper by Mirko Novák, Egypt and the Levant 14, 2004." *Ägypten und Levante/Egypt and the Levant* 17: 221-239.

Braun, Eliot. 2003. "South Levantine Encounters with Ancient Egypt at the Beginning of the Third Millennium." In *Ancient Perspectives on Egypt*, eds. Roger Matthews and Cornelia Roemer, 21-37. London: University College London Press.

Breasted, James Henry, ed. and trans. 2001. *Ancient Records of Egypt*. Vols. 2 and 3, *The Eighteenth Dynasty* and *The Nineteenth Dynasty*. Chicago: University of Illinois Press.

Frankfort, Henri. 1996. *The Art and Architecture of the Ancient Orient*. New Haven, Connecticut: Yale University Press.

Grajetzki, Wolfram. 2009. *The Middle Kingdom of Ancient Egypt*. London: Duckworth.

Haywood, John. 2005. *The Penguin Historical Atlas of Ancient Civilizations*. London: Penguin.

Herodotus. 2003. *The Histories*. Translated by Aubrey de Sélincourt. London: Penguin Books.

Kuhrt, Amélie. 2010. *The Ancient Near East: c. 3000-330 BCE*. 2 vols. London: Routledge.

Lichtheim, Miriam, ed. 2006. *Ancient Egyptian Literature*. Vol. 1, *The Old and Middle Kingdoms*. Los Angeles: University of California Press.

Malamat, Abraham. 1971. "Mari." *Biblical Archaeologist* 34: 1-22.

Mieroop, Marc van de. 2007. *A History of the Ancient Near East: ca. 3000-323 BCE*. 2nd ed. London: Blackwell.

Moran, William L., ed. and trans. 1992. *The Amarna Letters*. Baltimore: John Hopkins University Press.

Munn-Rankin, J. M. 1956. "Diplomacy in Western Asia in the Early Second Millennium B.C. *Iraq"* 18: 68-110.

Novák, Mirko. 2004. "The Chronology of the Royal Palace of Qatna." *Ägypten und Levante/Egypt and the Levant* 14: 299-317.

Pfälzner, Peter. 2009. "Königreich Qatna – ein 'Global Player" im alten Orient." *Archäologie in Deutschland* 5: 12-17.

Pitard, Wayne T. 2001. "Before Israel: Syria-Palestine in the Bronze Age." In *The Oxford History of the Biblical World*. Edited by Michael Coogan, 25-57. Oxford: Oxford University Press.

Pritchard, James B, ed. 1992. *Ancient Near Eastern Texts Relating to the Old Testament*. 3rd ed. Princeton, New Jersey: Princeton University Press.

Redford, Donald B. 1992. *Egypt, Canaan, and Israel in Ancient Times*. Princeton, New Jersey: Princeton University Press.

Sasson, Jack M., ed. 2015. *From the Mari Archives: An Anthology of Old Babylonian Letters*. Winona Lake, Indiana: Eisenbrauns.

Thomason, Allison Karmel. 2009. "Beyond Babylon: Art, Trade, and Diplomacy in the Second Millennium B.C.E.: An Exhibit at the Metropolitan Museum of Art, New York." *Near Eastern Archaeology* 72: 51-54.

Free Books by Charles River Editors

We have brand new titles available for free most days of the week. To see which of our titles are currently free, click on this link.

Discounted Books by Charles River Editors

We have titles at a discount price of just 99 cents everyday. To see which of our titles are currently 99 cents, click on this link.

CPSIA information can be obtained
at www.ICGtesting.com
Printed in the USA
LVHW061437270421
685706LV00020B/759